Small Animals
of North America
coloring book

Elizabeth
A. McClelland

Dover Publications, Inc.
New York

Publisher's Note

All the animals in this book are mammals: hair-covered, warm-blooded animals that nurse their young with milk, the vast majority of them having four feet and a tail. Though the United States and Canada also possess such large and imposing mammals as the bison and moose, by far the greater part of their mammals, and those most commonly seen, are much smaller. From the great variety of North American mammals smaller than deer, zoological illustrator Elizabeth A. McClelland has chosen 46 important examples and rendered them accurately and attractively for coloring. Not only are color indications supplied in the caption for each animal, but the artist has also provided full-color renderings of some 25 of the animals on the outer and inner covers of this book.

Other information given in the captions includes: common name of animal; scientific name of animal (in parentheses); in-dication of the classification of mammals to which it belongs; total average length of adult animal, always including tail; the type of landscape in which it is found; the parts of North America it normally inhabits; and occasionally some other data on its anatomy or habits.

Readers who desire further information on these and many other aspects of the animals are urged to consult *A Field Guide to the Mammals,* by William Henry Burt and Richard Philip Grossenheider (in the Peterson Field Guide Series), published by the Houghton Mifflin Company (3rd edition, 1976), a book that was the basis of the common and scientific names used here, and was in general a valuable source of information for the present volume. Also used in the preparation of the present captions was *Harper & Row's Complete Field Guide to North American Wildlife* (1981).

Badger (*Taxidea taxus*). Carnivore of the weasel family. About 30 inches long. Yellow-gray with white stripe, white cheeks, black feet. Active chiefly at night in prairies and deserts in U.S. Midwest and West, parts of southwest Canada, northern Mexico.

Southern Flying Squirrel (*Glaucomys volans*). Squirrels and their allies form one family of the order of rodents. This species of tree squirrel is about 10 inches long. Olive-brown above, white below. A layer of loose skin along its sides allows it to glide between trees. A nocturnal forest dweller in eastern half of U.S.

2

Red Squirrel (*Tamiasciurus hudsonicus*). About 14 inches long. Reddish or yellowish; in summer, a black line on sides. Lives in evergreen and hardwood forests and in swamps through most of Canada and Alaska, and in the Northeast, Great Lakes and Rockies areas of the U.S.

Western Gray Squirrel (*Sciurus griseus*). About 24 inches long. Gray; white belly; darker feet. Dweller in oak and pine forests on the West Coast of the U.S.

Tassel-eared Squirrel (*Sciurus aberti*). About 20 inches long. Reddish back; gray sides; black ear tufts; tail all or largely white. Inhabits yellow-pine forests in parts of Colorado, Utah, New Mexico and Arizona.

Thirteen-lined Ground Squirrel (*Citellus tridecemlineatus*). About 10 inches long. Brown with 13 whitish stripes or rows of spots. Lives in grasslands of central U.S. and adjacent parts of Canada.

Golden-mantled Squirrel (*Citellus lateralis*). About 12 inches long. Copper-colored head; lateral black-edged white stripe. Found in evergreen forests in western U.S. and a few parts of southwest Canada.

Least Chipmunk (*Eutamias minimus*). About 8 inches long. Tawny gray with dark stripes. Lives in sagebrush deserts or in forests in northwest U.S. and most of central and western Canada.

8

Armadillo (*Dasypus novemcinctus*). The only North American member of a family represented in South America by sloths and other species of armadillo. About 35 inches long. Covered with a horn-like material. Lives chiefly on insects. Found in wooded or brushy areas from Oklahoma and Texas to Florida and parts of Mexico near the Rio Grande.

Blacktail Prairie Dog (*Cynomys ludovicianus*). Prairie dogs are rodents of the squirrel family. This species is about 16 inches long. Yellowish with black-tipped tail. Lives in burrow "towns" on prairies from Montana to Texas.

Bushytail Woodrat (*Neotoma cinerea*). Woodrats, or "packrats," are rodents of the mouse-and-vole family. This species is about 15 inches long. Gray to black with white hind feet. Lives in mountainous areas in northwest U.S. and British Columbia.

11

Ringtail (*Bassariscus astutus*). Carnivore related to the raccoon. About 30 inches long. Yellow-gray body, whitish and brownish rings on tail. Hunts at night in shrubby areas of southwest U.S. and Mexico.

12

Ord Kangaroo Rat (*Dipodomys ordi*). Rodents of the pocket-mouse family. About 10 inches long. Dark and white tail stripes. Nocturnal in sandy areas in western half of U.S.

Kit Fox (*Vulpes macrotis*). Foxes are carnivores of the dog family. This species is about 30 inches long. Gray body; whitish belly; black-tipped tail; large ears. Night hunter in desert areas from California to Texas and parts of northern Mexico.

Raccoon (*Procyon lotor*). About 40 inches long. Grizzled body; white and black tail rings; black "mask." Lives near water in wooded regions over most of U.S., southern areas of Canada, Mexico.

Red Fox (*Vulpes fulva*). About 40 inches long. Reddish yellow; white belly and tail tip; black legs. Inhabits forests and open country through most of North America north of Mexico.

Gray Fox (*Urocyon cinereoargenteus*). About 45 inches long. Grizzled body, black stripe down tail. Nocturnal hunter in open forests and shrubby regions through most of U.S. (not in northwest quadrant) and Mexico.

Longtail Weasel (*Mustela frenata*). About 15 inches long. Brown; yellow-white belly; black tail tip.
Mainly nocturnal. Lives near water in most of U.S., parts of southern Canada, Mexico.

Mink (*Mustela vison*). Weasel family. About 25 inches long. Deep brown with white patch on chin. Mainly nocturnal. Lives near water throughout Alaska, Canada and U.S. (except Southwest).

Marten (*Martes americana*). Weasel family. About 25 inches long. Yellow-brown with buff patch on throat and breast. Mainly nocturnal in evergreen forests (West) or cedar swamps (East) through most of Alaska and Canada and small areas of northwest U.S.

Black-footed Ferret (*Mustela nigripes*). Weasel family. About 22 inches long. Yellow-brown body; black on forehead, tail tip and feet. Usually found in the "towns" of prairie dogs, its chief prey. Same range as prairie dogs (see no. 10).

Snowshoe Hare (*Lepus americanus*). Rabbits, hares and pikas form an order of mammals of their own. The snowshoe hare is about 18 inches long. Dark brown in summer, white in winter. Nocturnal in swamps and forests through most of Alaska and Canada, and in adjacent parts of U.S. (Northeast, Northwest and Great Lakes).

Eastern Cottontail (*Sylvilagus floridanus*). About 17 inches long. Brownish or grayish with white tail. Brushy areas or open forest through most of U.S. (not in northern New England or Far West) and parts of Mexico.

Blacktail Jackrabbit (*Lepus californicus*). About 20 inches long. Gray-brown; black on ear tips and tail top. Prairie and desert dweller in southwest U.S. and adjacent states, and parts of Mexico.

24

River Otter (*Lutra canadensis*). Carnivore of the weasel family. About 45 inches long. Dark brown. Webbed feet. Lives near water through most of North America north of Mexico.

Muskrat (*Ondatra zibethica*). Rodent of the mouse-and-vole family. About 25 inches long. Dark brown, hairless black tail. Builds houses in bodies of water throughout most of North America north of Mexico.

Beaver (*Castor canadensis*). Beavers form their own family of rodents. About 40 inches long. Dark brown; paddle-shaped hairless tail. Builds dams in streams or houses in lakes. Mainly nocturnal. Found just about everywhere in North America north of Mexico.

Spotted Skunk (*Spilogale putorius*). Skunks are carnivores of the weasel family. This species is about 22 inches long. Black with white spots and stripes. Night forager in grassy, brushy or wooded areas in Mexico and in most of U.S. south of the Ohio and west of the Mississippi.

28

Striped Skunk (*Mephitis mephitis*). About 25 inches long. Black with white stripes. Habits and habitats similar to those of spotted skunk, but ranges all over U.S. and southern Canada.

Eastern Mole (*Scalopus aquaticus*). Moles form a family within the order of insect-eaters. This species is about 7 inches long. Fur varies from gray to brown to golden; hairless tail. Lives in fields, meadows and gardens through most of U.S. (not extreme Northeast) from the Atlantic to the Rockies.

Woodchuck (*Marmota monax*). Also known as groundhog; a rodent of the squirrel family. Brown, darker feet. Woodlands and brushlands. Most of eastern half of U.S. (not deep South) and most of Canada (not far North).

Yellowbelly Marmot (*Marmota flaviventris*). A close relative of the woodchuck. About 25 inches long. Yellow-brown body; yellow belly; white blaze between the eyes. Lives in rocky, elevated areas in western U.S. and parts of Alberta and British Columbia.

Bobcat (*Lynx rufus*). Carnivore of the cat family. About 35 inches long. Brownish with black spots and stripes; tail has black tip. Shrubby areas (West) or swamps and forests (East). Nocturnal. Mexico, most of U.S. (not in parts of South and Midwest), southern edge of Canada.

Opossum (*Didelphis marsupialis*). The only North America marsupial (premature young develop in pouch, as with kangaroos, etc.). Up to 40 inches long. Gray; white face; black ears and tail (with white end). Farmlands and woodlands. Mainly nocturnal. Eastern two-thirds of U.S. and Pacific coast, parts of Mexico.

34

Porcupine (*Erethizon dorsatum*). Separate family of rodents. About 30 inches long. Black; quills on rump and tail. Nocturnal forest dweller through most of Alaska and Canada and western third of U.S.

Shorttail Shrew (*Blarina brevicauda*). Shrews form one of the two North American families of insect-eaters (moles are the other). This species is about 5 inches long. Dark gray; no external ears; tiny eyes. Lives in a wide range of habitats in eastern half of U.S. and adjacent portions of Canada.

Valley Pocket Gopher (*Thomomys bottae*). Pocket gophers are a distinct family of rodents. This species is up to 10 inches long; size varies geographically. Coloration also varies from whitish to blackish. Inhabits valleys and meadows from California to western Texas and adjacent parts of Mexico.

Deer Mouse (*Peromyscus maniculatus*). Rodent of the mouse-and-vole family. About 9 inches long. Gray to brown color variations; tail dark above, white below; feet white. Inhabits dry-land areas through most of Canada, some of Alaska, most of U.S. (not Southeast), parts of Mexico.

ABOVE: **Western Harvest Mouse** (*Reithrodontomys megalotis*). In the mouse-and-vole family. About 6 inches long. Gray to brown. Grassland and desert over most of western half of U.S., into Mexico. BELOW: **Hispid Pocket Mouse** (*Perognathus hispidus*). In the pocket-mouse family. About 9 inches long. Fur a yellow-brown mix. Prairies and roadsides in central U.S. from Dakotas to Texas and Arizona, into Mexico.

Southern Bog Lemming (*Synaptomys cooperi*). In the mouse-and-vole family. About 5 inches long. Brownish gray. Bogs and meadows in northeast quadrant of U.S. and adjacent parts of Canada.

Pika (*Ocotona princeps*). In same order of mammals as rabbits and hares. About 8 inches long. Gray to brown. Mountain dweller in western U.S., Alberta, British Columbia.

Coyote (*Canis latrans*). Carnivore; dog family. About 50 inches long. Gray; legs and ears rust-colored. Mainly nocturnal in open country in Alaska, western and southern Canada, Mexico, and most of U.S. (not in Southeast).

42

Peccary (*Pecari angulatus*). A family of its own within the order of even-toed hoofed mammals (this order also includes swine, deer, sheep, etc.). About 36 inches long. Black and gray fur. Semidesert areas. Parts of Arizona, New Mexico, Texas; Mexico, continuing into South America.   43

Meadow Vole (*Microtus pennsylvanicus*). About 7 inches long. Gray to dark brown geographical variants. Grasslands and near bodies of water throughout Alaska and Canada and in northern third of U.S.

Big Brown Bat (*Eptesicus fuscus*). Bats form a separate order of mammals. This species has a wingspread of about 12 inches. Pale to dark brown. Nocturnal. Lives in caves, hollow trees, wooded areas throughout U.S., in Canadian provinces adjacent to U.S., Mexico. 45

Index